Instant Marketing Success

10 New and Radical Strategies to Help Your Business Thrive

by Elena Nugent

COPYRIGHT AND DISCLAIMER

This material is copyright. No part, in whole or in part, may be reproduced by any process, or any other exclusive right exercised, without the permission of www.resultsch.com © 2017

Elena Nugent

Published by:
Leader Publishing Worldwide
19 Axford Bay
Port Moody, BC V3H 3R4
Tel: 1 888 294 9151
Fax: 1 877 575 9151
Website: www.noresults-nofee.com

DISCLAIMER AND/OR LEGAL NOTICES:
While every attempt has been made to verify information provided in this book, neither the author nor the publisher assumes any responsibility for any errors, omissions or inaccuracies.

Any slights of people or organizations are unintentional. If advice concerning legal or related matters is needed, the services of a qualified professional should be sought. This book is not intended as a source of legal or accounting advice. You should be aware of any laws which govern business transactions or other business practices in your state or province.

The income statements and examples are not intended to represent or guarantee that everyone will achieve the same results. Each individual's success will be determined by his or her desire, dedication, effort, and motivation. There are no guarantees you will duplicate the results stated here, you recognize that any business endeavor has inherent risk for loss of capital.

Any reference to any persons or business, whether living or deceased, existing or defunct, is purely coincidental.

PRINTED IN THE USA

DEDICATION

I would like to dedicate this book to my cool family- loving husband Gerald, amazing son Arseni, and beautiful Mom Nina. Thank you for your support and unconditional love for me. I hope I make you proud.

CONTENTS

Chapter 1	...	Creating a Powerful Offer
Chapter 2	...	Copywriting for Profits
Chapter 3	...	Profiting from Internet Marketing
Chapter 4	...	How to Profit from Direct Mail
Chapter 5	...	How to Use Advertising for Immediate Profits
Chapter 6	...	Systemizing Your Business and Developing Effective Processes
Chapter 7	...	Generating an Unlimited Amount of Leads for Your Business
Chapter 8	...	Use Goal Setting Effectively
Chapter 9	...	How to Use Testimonials and Profit from Social Proof
Chapter 10	...	Profits and Leads through Host Beneficiary Relationships

INTRODUCTION

This is the first page, but by opening this book you have already taken an important step towards increasing the success of your business. Congratulations in your quest to enhance your business and marketing skills.

When I put pen to paper or keyboard to word document, I found myself with an enormous amount of useful marketing material I've used since 1992. This experience is drawn from many different business entities including work with an International Lending Institution overseas, Project Manager for a small East Coast firm; Strategic Communications Manager with a Fortune 500 company; and a small business owner. The strategies I talk about in this book are still in place at these companies.

Even though I truly believe we are all 1 or 2 great marketing ideas away from more sales opportunities than we can fully imagine, I believe the first two chapters are as important as the following eight. The strategies in this book - when implemented with strategy and care - are guaranteed to make you more money with less effort. These are strategies that have helped businesses just like yours make hundreds of thousands of dollars - including your competitors.

This is the reason I have dedicated my life to Business Consulting. Since starting my company to provide direction for small business operators, I have been literally overwhelmed with the demand for marketing, structure, accountability and for the need to have small business operators surrounding themselves with someone that cares and to provide a proper and profitable third party perspective.

As you follow the book and read the principles to follow, remember it does not matter what industry nor type of business you operate. What matters is that you grasp the heart of the principles, the underlying lessons and strategies, that can help grow any operation in any category of business imaginable.

The best time to start is NOW, not tomorrow, not next week or next year.

Yours in success,

Elena Nugent

PS. If you would like to arrange a meeting to get a profitable third party perspective on your business, please send an email to info@resultsch.com and we will gladly point you in the right direction.

To learn how to avoid the 3 key mistakes all small business owners make, visit www.resultsorientedcoaching.com

1

Creating a Powerful Offer

I'm not going to beat around the bush on this one:

Your offer is the granite foundation of your marketing campaign.

Get it right, and everything else will fall into place. Your headline will grab readers, your copy will sing, your ad layout will hardly matter, and you will have customers running to your door.

Get it wrong, and even the best looking, best-written campaign will sink like the Titanic.

A powerful offer is an irresistible offer. It's an offer that gets your audience frothing at the mouth and clamoring over each other all the way to your door. An offer that makes your readers pick up the phone and open their wallets.

Irresistible offers make your potential customers think, "I'd be crazy not to take him up on that," or "An offer like this doesn't come around very often." They instill a sense of emotion, of desire, and ultimately, urgency.

Make it easy for customers to purchase from you the first time, and spend your time keeping them coming back.

I'll say it again: **get it right, and everything else will fall into place.**

The Crux of Your Marketing Campaign

As you work your way through this program, you will find that nearly every chapter discusses the importance of a powerful offer as related to your marketing strategy or promotional campaign.

There's a reason for this. The powerful offer is more often than not the reason a customer will open their wallets. It is how you generate leads, and then convert them into loyal customers. The more dramatic, unbelievable, and valuable the offer is the more dramatic and unbelievable the response will be.

Many companies spend thousands of dollars on impressive marketing campaigns in glossy magazines and big city newspapers. They send massive direct mail campaigns on a regular basis; yet don't receive an impressive or massive response rate.

These companies do not yet understand that simply providing information on their company and the benefits of their product is not enough to get customers to act. There is no reason to pick up the phone or visit the store, *right now*.

Your powerful, irresistible offer can:
- Increase leads
- Drive traffic to your website or business
- Move old product
- Convert leads into customers
- Build your customer database

What Makes a Powerful Offer?

A powerful offer is one that makes the most people respond, and take action. It gets people running to spend money on your product or service.

Powerful offers nearly always have an element of *urgency* and of *scarcity*. They give your audience a reason to act immediately, instead of put it off until a later date.

Urgency relates to time. The offer is only available until a certain date, during a certain period of the day, or if you act within a few hours of seeing the ad. The customer needs to act now to take advantage of the offer.

Scarcity related to quantity. There are only a certain number of customers who will be able to take advantage of the offer. There may be a limited number of spaces, a limited number of products, or simply a limited number of people the business will provide the offer to. Again, this requires that customer acts immediately to reap the high value for low cost.

Powerful offers also:

Offer great value. Customers perceive the offer as having great value – more than a single product on its own, or the product at its regular price. It is clear that the offer takes the reader's needs and wants into consideration.

Make sense to the reader. They are simple and easy to understand if read quickly. Avoid percentages – use half off or 2 for 1 instead of 50% off. There are no "catches" or requirements; no fine print.

Seem logical. The offer doesn't come out of thin air. There is a logical reason behind it – a holiday, end of season, anniversary celebration, or new product. People can get suspicious of offers that seem "too good to be true" and have no apparent purpose.

Provide a premium. The offer provides something extra to the customer, like a free gift, or free product or service. They feel they are getting something extra for no extra cost. Premiums are perceived to have more value than discounts.

Remember that when your target market reads your offer, they will be asking the following questions:

1. What are you offering me?
2. What's in it for me?
3. What makes me sure I can believe you?
4. How much do I have to pay for it?

The Most Powerful Types of Offers

Decide what kind of offer will most effectively achieve your objectives. Are you trying to generate leads, convert customers, build a database, move old product off the shelves, or increase sales?

Consider what type of offer will be of most value to your ideal customers – what offer will make them act quickly.

Free Offer

This type of offer asks customers to act immediately in exchange for something free. This is a good strategy to use to build a customer database or mailing list. Offer a free consultation, free consumer report, or other item of low cost to you but of high perceived value.

You can also advertise the value of the item you are offering for free. For example, act now and you'll receive a free consultation, worth $75 dollars. This will dramatically increase your lead generation, and allow you to focus on conversion when the customer comes through the door or picks up the phone.

The Value Added Offer

Add additional services or products that cost you very little, and combine them with other items to increase their attractiveness. This increases the perception of value in the customer's mind, which will justify increasing the price of a product or service without incurring extra hard costs to your business.

Package Offer

Package your products or services together in a logical way to increase the perceived value as a whole. Discount the value of the package by a small margin, and position it as a "start-up kit" or "special package." By packaging goods of mixed values, you will be able to close more high-value sales. For example: including a free desk-jet printer with every computer purchase.

Premium Offer

Offer a bonus product or service with the purchase of another. This strategy will serve your bottom line much better than discounting. This includes 2 for 1 offers, offers that include free gifts, and in-store credit with purchases over a specific dollar amount.

Urgency Offer

As I mentioned above, offers that include an element of urgency enjoy a better response rate, as there is a reason for your customers to act immediately. Give the offer a deadline or limit the number of spots available.

Guarantee Offer

Offer to take the risk of making a purchase away from your customers. Guarantee the performance or results of your product or service, and offer to compensate the customer with their money back if they are not satisfied. This will help overcome any fear or reservations about your product, and make it more likely for your leads to become customers.

Create Your Powerful Offer

1. Pick a single product or service.

Focus on only one product or service – or one product or service *type* – at a time. This will keep your offer clear, simple, and easy to understand. This can be an area of your business you wish to grow, or old product that you need to move off the shelves.

2. Decide what you want your customers to do.

What are you looking to achieve from your offer? If it is to generate more leads, then you'll need your customer to contact you. If it is to quickly sell old product, you'll need your customer to come into the store and buy it. Do you want them to visit your website? Sign up for your newsletter? How long do they have to act? Be clear about your call to action, and state it clearly in your offer.

3. Dream up the biggest, best offer.

First, think of the biggest, best things you could offer your customers – regardless of cost and ability. Don't limit yourself to a single type of offer, combine several types of offers to increase value. Offer a premium, plus a guarantee, with a package offer. Then take a look at what you've created, and make the necessary changes so it is realistic.

4. Run the numbers.

Finally, make sure the offer will leave you with some profit – or at least allow you to break even. You don't want to publish an outrageous offer that will generate a tremendous number of leads, but leave you broke. Remember that each customer has an acquisition cost, as well as a lifetime value. The amount of their first purchase may allow you to break even, but the amount of their subsequent purchases may make you a lovely profit.

2

Copywriting for Profits

When it comes to marketing, we all know that *what* you say is just as important as *how* you say it.

In fact, I would argue that how you say something is even more important than what you have to say.

Think about it. The whole purpose of communicating is to get a message to its intended audience. In business, this means telling your target market why they should buy your product or service, and why they should buy it from you.

You could have the best, most irresistible offer out there, but if you can't get your audience to pay attention to your ad, it's worthless. You may offer the solution to their biggest frustration, but if you can't get them to read beyond your headline, it means nothing.

Effective copywriting gets your message to your target audience and then leads them to act. **Effective copywriting gets you the sale.**

Good Copy, Bad Copy

There are a number of misconceptions out there when it comes to copywriting for marketing collateral.

The first is that good copy must be clever (or witty, funny, dramatic, ironic, etc.). People get wrapped up in the idea that their ads need to compete with the ads on the pages of Vanity Fair – or the New York Times. They feel that their campaign needs to be littered with clever words that allude to the pop culture of the day, or position their company as "hip" or sophisticated.

This, in my experience, is rubbish.

The second assumption most business owners make is that good copy is the backbone of a successful ad or marketing campaign. I can't tell you how many good copywriters I've seen take the blame for a bad offer, or poorly positioned product.

The third misconception is that you need to be a good writer to write good copy. Or, if you're not a good writer, that you need to spend thousands of dollars on a copywriter for each of your marketing pieces.

That's rubbish, too.

So, then, what is good copy? And how do you write it?

The Purpose of Your Copy

Here are the key points you need to remember when crafting your advertisements:

a. A good headline *gets your readers to read the first sentence.*
b. A good first sentence *gets your readers to read the second sentence.*
c. And so on and on until the end of your marketing piece; or, the close of the sale.

Simple, isn't it?

The copy in your marketing materials is intended to persuade your audience to buy what you have to offer – one sentence at a time. Once you understand that copywriting is persuasive writing, not creative or technical writing, you will have much more success with your copywriting efforts.

Persuasive copy can be written in a number of ways – which we will discuss later in the section – but always includes:

- a compelling, shocking, or gripping headline
- a strong promise
- a heavy focus on benefits, not features
- proof to back up your claims

Compelling writing slowly builds a case, and leads the reader down a specific path to the final destination: the sale. The argument or message is built up over several sentences, or paragraphs, until the reader is primed and ready for the question.

For example, if you came right out in your headline and said, "Buy Tommy's Sprockets to Solve Your Problems", your highly skeptical audience would not give your ad a second glance. You've asked for the sale right up front, before building some trust and slowly persuading your readers.

However, if you took the time to build your case, the ad would read something like this:

DON'T BUY ANOTHER SPROCKET UNTIL YOU READ THIS

Did you know that the average sprocket is made with only 25% authentic materials? To speed up production and reduce costs, sprocket manufacturing over the last decade has begun to rely heavily on artificial materials.

Would you trust the safety of your family to a product that reduces quality to preserve profit?

At Tommy's Sprockets, we put the safety of your family first. Our sprockets are stronger and safer, because we still make them the old fashioned way – with 100% authentic materials and a lifetime guarantee.

Sure, they cost a little more than the average sprocket, but how much more would you pay for the safety of your family?

This ad isn't going to win any Pulitzer Prizes, but it doesn't need to. It engages the audience, communicates benefits, supports with features, and paints a compelling argument.

Headlines

Headlines are so crucial to the copywriting in your advertisement or sales letter that they deserve an entire section in this chapter.

Your headline is the first chance you have to make an impression on your target audience. Quite possibly, it is also your only chance. Without a headline that grabs your reader by the neck and focuses on what you have to say, the remainder of your ad is useless.

That's why even the greatest copywriters spend 50% of their time on the headline, and 50% on the rest of the copy.

With that in mind, it's important to note that your headline needs to do more than simply grab the attention of your potential readers. It also needs to tell them why they should care – your headline needs to send a full message that informs and encourages them to read onwards.

The most effective way to do this is to make an offer or promise to the reader that makes the time they invest in reading your ad worthwhile.

Seems like a lot for 8 to 10 words, doesn't it?

Headline Length

The general understanding when it comes to headline length is the shorter the better. But this comes from headline creation for newspapers and magazines, where space is crunched and nothing is up for sale.

In fact, based on studies done in the direct mail industry, 40% to 50% of the most effective headlines are more than eight words in length – meaning there are really no hard and fast rules for headline length.

Another marketing example of headline length is in sales letters. I'm sure you've seen headlines in sales letters that actually comprise small paragraphs. This is the opposite way of thinking from newspaper headlines, but in this medium it works.

The point is, if you need more than eight words to get your message across, then use more.

Headline Readers: The 80/20 Rule

According to readership statistics, eight out of 10 people read headlines, but only two of 10 will read the rest of the advertisement or letter. This proves the importance of crafting powerful, meaningful headlines. It also proves that an effective headline is the golden key to getting the rest of the piece read.

So, it would stand to reason that the better your headline, the higher the chances of improving the averages in these statistics.

Headline Types

Direct Headlines simply state the offer or proposition in as clear a manner as possible. *All winter clothing 30% off.*

News Headlines typically announce a new product or piece of information and mimic a headline you would read in a newspaper. *Jonny launches new line of improved sprockets.*

The Question Headline asks a question that the reader can relate to or would be compelled to read on to find the answer. *Do you want clearer skin?*

The 'How to' Headline tells the reader the body copy or product will explain step by step instructions for something of interest to the reader. *How to save $1,000 in energy costs this year.*

Command Headline is one of the strongest headline types, and commands the reader to do something. *Make your dreams come true today.*

The '7 Reasons Why' Headline tells the reader the body copy will include 7 (or another number less than seven) points that will either back up a claim or illustrate product benefits. *7 reasons why your teenagers won't listen to you.*

Testimonial Headlines leverages the power of outsider and expert opinion and quotes them directly in the headline. *"Tommy's sprockets have changed my life" says Brad Pitt.*

In summary, your headline should:

- Be immediately engaging
- Be useful and relevant to the reader
- Convey information
- Trigger an emotional reaction
- Include an offer
- Intrigue your audience

Strategies for Better Copywriting

Simplify, Simplify, Simplify

Good copy is written in clear, simple language with short sentence structure. It's conversational and reads like you are speaking to a friend or colleague.

Important points – like benefits – are listed in numbered or bullet format and traditional grammar is sacrificed for brevity.

Always read your copy before you finalize it and take out any unnecessary words. Find the shortest way to communicate the most information.

Be More Persuasive

Persuasion is an important technique for structuring your copy. While there is no clear formula for any type of copywriting, persuasive copy consistently includes the following elements:

- Has a reader focus from the very beginning
- Each paragraph or section supports the main argument
- Is highly specific and provides proof to support claims
- Includes credible proof like statistics and expert opinion
- Returns the focus to the reader as often as possible

Persuasive writing convinces the reader that they should believe what you say and do you what you say, and that there is something in it for them if they do. Again, there is no formula for this and no clear content rules, but there are some strategies you can use to make your writing more persuasive.

Repeat your point over and over

Repetition is a powerful and essential tool when crafting persuasive copy. It often will take several attempts at communicating before someone truly understands what you're saying. The benefit is that the more you say it, and the more ways you say it, the more likely your audience will believe it.

Of course, don't literally repeat yourself verbatim in your copy. Use a few different techniques to communicate the same point – for example, state it directly, tell a story, then repeat it again in your summary.

Give them reasons why

Backup your claims and requests with good reasons and leverage the power of the word 'because.' Studies have proven that even if the reason doesn't make any sense, or isn't directly related to the claim, people will be more likely to believe you simply based on the fact you backed up what you had to say.

Make comparisons to prove a point

Use the power of metaphors, analogies, and similes in your writing. This gives you an opportunity to relate the point you are trying to make directly to something the reader can relate to and understands to be true.

This is effective for making comparisons between like subjects, as well as unlike subjects, depending on the point you are trying to make.

Answer silent objections

Show that you understand the reader's point of view and thought process by answering questions you know they will be considering in their minds.

While you will not be able to address all potential objections in a single piece, or think of all potential objections your reader may raise, you can definitely dispute the most common arguments against what you are claiming.

Tell a story

Storytelling is an effective technique to use in all aspects of your copywriting. People relate to the experiences of others, and strive to learn from or compare themselves to the characters in the anecdotes. The story ends up doing the persuading for you.

Focus on Benefits

This is an obvious aspect of your messaging that you will feature in every piece you write, but it's not always easy to do well. Many writers end up featuring a slew of fake benefits instead of real ones.

Real benefits are things the reader actually cares about. For example, if you sold cough syrup you would want to explain how it eases the cold or flu symptoms, and not that it cures the illness. The symptoms are what are bothering the reader – that's what aspect of the product they care about and will make their purchase based on.

Make a Better Offer

Compel the reader to act with a stronger offer – one that they just can't possibly refuse. Make one that seems just believable enough to take action and reap the rewards.

A strong offer features a product or service with a high perceived value for a low cost. It could be a package of products offered for a lower price than the sum of the individual products, or a "free gift" with purchase.

Use Words that Work

Another misconception when it comes to copywriting is that it needs to be 100% unique. I'm not saying you should blatantly plagiarize other writer's work, but you should definitely pay attention to what works.

This includes how an ad is structured, how a point is made, or the hierarchy of the content. It also includes word choice. Certain words in marketing have been proven to have a stronger impact on general consumers than others.

There are tools that are easily available to you that will provide a list or database of effective words for use in advertising. Research online or invest in a software programs like Glyphus to use as a resource.

Offer a Guarantee

A guarantee is another technique that will compel a potential customer to take action. A strong guarantee takes the risk involved in purchase decisions away from the customer, and puts it on the seller.

Tell your customer that if your product or service doesn't deliver the performance or results you have promised, you'll give them their money back or compensate them in a way that will make it right.

3

Profiting from Internet Marketing

Is your business online? If not, it should be.

The internet is today's primary consumer research tool. If your business does not have an online presence, it is harder for customers to find and choose your business over the competition. With over 73% of North Americans online, it is no wonder that individuals and businesses in all industries are looking to the internet to enhance their marketing strategies.

Luckily, it has never been easier to establish and maintain a comprehensive online presence. Internet marketing, also referred to as online marketing, online advertising or e-marketing, is the fastest growing medium for marketing.

But it is not just company websites that users are viewing. Blogs, consumer reviews, chat rooms and a variety of social media are growing rapidly in popularity.

The internet is a very powerful tool for businesses if used strategically and effectively. It can be a cost saving alternative to traditional marketing approaches, and may be the most effective way to communicate with your target consumer.

A major advantage of the internet is that you are always open. Users can access your business 24 hours a day, 7 days a week, and depending on your business and the purpose of the website, visitors can also purchase goods at any time.

Internet Marketing for Everyone

The internet is a great way to create product and brand awareness, develop relationships with consumers and share and exchange information. You can't afford not be taking advantage of online marketing opportunities because your competition is likely already there.

Internet marketing can take on many different forms. By creating maintaining a website for your business, you are reaching out to a new consumer base. You can have full control over the messaging that users are receiving and has a global reach.

Internet marketing can be very cost effective. If you have a strong email database of your customers, an e-newsletter may be cheaper and more effective than post mail. You can deliver time sensitive materials immediately and can update your subscribers instantaneously.

Top 10 Websites (Globally Jan 2017)

1.	Google	7.	Wikipedia
2.	Facebook	8.	Tencent QQ
3.	YouTube	9.	LinkedIn
4.	Windows Live	10.	Taobao.com
5.	Yahoo	11.	Twitter
6.	Baidu.com		

To learn the 3 biggest mistakes all business owners make and how to avoid them, visit www.resultsorientedcoaching.com

You will notice that half of these websites are search engines. An increasing number of consumers are first researching products, services and companies online, whether it be to compare products, complete a sale, or look for a future employer. Most people in the 18-35 age group obtain all of their information online—including news, weather, product research, etc. The remaining sites are interactive sites where users can upload information for social networking, or information sharing.

Internet Marketing Strategies

Internet marketing – like all other elements of your marketing campaign – needs to have clear goals and objectives. Creating brand and product awareness will not happen overnight so it is important to budget accordingly, ensuring there is money set aside for maintenance of the website and analytics.

Be flexible with ideas and options—do your research first, try out different options, then test and measure the results. Metrics and evaluations can be updated almost immediately and should be monitored regularly. By keeping an eye out for what online marketing strategies are working and which are not, it will be easier to create a balanced portfolio of marketing techniques. You might find that in certain geographical areas, certain marketing strategies are more effective than others.

This list is by no means the full extent of options available for marketing online, but it is a good place to start when deciding which options are best suited to your company.

Create a website

The primary use for the internet is information seeking, so you should provide consumers with information about your company first hand. You have more control over your branding and messaging and can also collect visitor information to determine what types of internet users are accessing your website.

Search Engine Optimization

Since search engines comprise 50% of the most visited sites globally, you can go through your website to make it more search engine friendly with the aim to increase your organic search listing. An organic search listing refers to listings in search engine results that appear in order or relevance to the entered search terms.

You may wish to repeat key words multiple times throughout your website and write the copy on your site not only with the end reader in mind, but also search engines.

Remember when you design your website that any text that appears in Flash format is not recognized by search engines. If your entire website is built on a Flash platform, then you will have a poor organic search listing.

Price Per Click Advertising

If you find that visitors access your website after searching for it first on a search engine, then it may be beneficial to advertise on these websites and bid on keywords associated with your company.

These advertisements will appear at the top of the page or along the left side of the search results on a search engine. You can have control over the specific geographic area you wish to target, set a monthly budget and have the option on only being charged when a user clicks on your link.

Online Directories

Listing your business in an online directory can be an inexpensive and effective online marketing strategy.

However, you need to be able to distinguish your company from the plethora of competitors that may exist. Likely, you will need to complement this strategy with other brand awareness campaigns.

Online Ads (i.e. banner ads on other websites)

These advertisements can have positive or negative effects based on the reputation and consumer perception of the website on which you are advertising. These ads should be treated similar to print ads you may place in local newspapers or other publications.

Online Videos

With the growing popularity of sites such as You Tube, it is evident that people love researching online and being able to find video clips of the information they are seeking. Depending on your small business, you may want to upload informational videos or tutorials about your products or services.

Blogging

Blogging can be a fun and interactive way to communicate with users. A blog is traditionally a website maintained by an individual user that has regular entries, similar to a diary. These entries can be commentary, descriptions of events, pictures, videos, and more. Companies can use blogging as a way to keep users updated on current information and allow them to post comments on your blog. If blogging is something you wish to invest in, make sure that it is regularly updated and monitored.

Top 10 Mistakes to Avoid

Failure to measure ROI

Which metrics are you using? Are your visitors actually motivated to purchase or sign up? If the benefits of your online campaign are not greater than the costs incurred, then you may wish to re-evaluate your strategy.

Poor Web Design

This can leave a poor impression of your company on the visitor. A poor design could result in frustration on the visitors' part if they are not able to easily find what they went on your site to search for and also does not build trust. If consumers do not trust your company or your website, you will not be able to complete the sale and develop a longer relationship with that customer. You also need to include privacy protection and security when building trust.

This also includes ensuring all information on the website is current and having customer service available if users are experiencing difficulty or cannot find the information they are seeking. This could be as simple as providing a 'Contact Us' email or phone number for support.

Becoming locked into an advertising strategy early

Remember your marketing mix when creating a marketing strategy and avoid putting all of your eggs in one basket. Online marketing is a very valuable tool, but depending on your business and your target markets, other marketing campaigns may be the best option for you. Especially if this is your first time making a significant investment into your online sector, you want to remain flexible and able to adapt your strategy based off feedback received by researching and analyzing different options.

Acting without researching

Similar to becoming locked into an advertising strategy early, this mistake implies not dutifully testing and researching different online marketing options. For example, if your target consumer is aged 65+ and you are spending all of your marketing efforts into creating a blogging website (where the average ages of bloggers are 18-35), then you are likely not going to have a successful campaign.

Assuming more visitors means more sales

You have to go back to your original goals and the purpose of your company. More visitors may not mean more sales if your website is used primarily for information and consumers purchase their products elsewhere. This is also vice versa. You could have an increase in sales without an increase in unique visitors if your current consumer base is very loyal and willing to spend lots of money.

Often people will collect information online about products they wish to purchase because it is easier to compare options, but they purchase in person. Even though shopping online is becoming quite popular, people still prefer to see and feel the physical product before purchasing.

Failing to follow up with customers that purchase

Return sales can account for up to 60% of total revenue. It's no wonder that organizations are always trying to maintain loyal customers and may have customer relationship management systems in place. It is easier to get a happy customer to purchase again than it is to get a new customer to purchase once.

Not incorporating online marketing into the business plan

By ensuring that your online marketing plan is fully integrated and accurately represents your organization's overall goals and objectives, the business plan will be more comprehensive and encompassing.

Trying to discover your own best practices

It is very beneficial to use trial and error to determine the best online strategy from your company, but do not be afraid to do your research and learn from what other have already figured out. There will be many cases where someone was in a very similar position as you and they may have some suggestions and secrets that they wish to share. Researching in advance can save a great deal of time and money.

Spending too much too fast

Although it may be cheaper than traditional marketing approaches, internet marketing does have its costs. You have to consider the software and hardware designs, maintenance, distribution, supply chain management, and the time that will be required. You don't want to spend your entire marketing budget all at once.

Getting distracted by metrics that are not relevant

As discussed in the following section, there are endless reports and measurables that you can analyze to determine the effectiveness of your campaign. You will need to establish which measurables are actually relevant to your marketing.

Testing and Measuring Online

As with any element of your marketing campaign, you will need to track your results and measure them against your investment. Otherwise, how will you know if your online marketing is successful?

These results - or metrics – need to be recorded and analyzed as to how they impact your overall return on investment.

Some examples of metrics are:

- New account setups
- Conversion rates
- Page stickiness
- Contact us form completion

Due to the popularity in online marketing and the importance of having a strong web presence, companies have demanded more sophisticated tracking tools and metrics for their online activities. It can be very difficult to not only know what to measure, but also HOW to measure.

Thankfully, it is easier than ever to get the information you need with the many types of software and services available, including Google Analytics, which are free and relatively accurate.

8 Metrics to Track

The following are the key measurables to watch for when testing and measuring your internet marketing efforts:

Conversions

How many leads has your online presence generated, and of those leads, how many were turned into sales? Ultimately, your campaign needs to have a positive impact on your business.

Regardless of the specific purpose of the campaign – from lead generation and service sign-up, to blog entries – you need to know how many customers are taking the desired action in response to your efforts. Your tracking tool will be able to provide you with this information

Spend

If you are not making a profit – or at least breaking even – from your internet marketing efforts, then you need to change your strategy. Redistribute your financial resources and reconsider your motives and objectives for your online campaign.

An easy way to do this analysis is to divide your total spend by conversions. This could also be broken down by product. You could also use tracking tool and view reports on the 'per visit value of every click,' from every type of source. Your sources can include organic/search engine referrals, direct visit (i.e. person typed your web address into their address bar), or email/newsletter.

Attention

You need to keep a close eye on how much attention you are getting on your website. One of the best ways to analyze this would be to compare unique visitors to page views per visit to time on site. How many people are visiting, how many pages they are viewing, what pages they are viewing, and how much time they are spending on the site.

A unique visitor is any one person who visits the website in a given amount of time. For example, if Evelyn visits her online banking website daily for an entire month, over that one month period, she is considered to be one unique visitor (not 30 visitors).

You may also want to incorporate referring source as well – the places online that refer customers to your website. You'll be able to determine what referring sources offer the 'best' visitors.

Top Referrals

Know who is doing the best job of referring clients to your website – and note how they are doing this. Is it the prominence of the link? Positioning? Reputation of the referring company?

Understanding where the majority of your visitors are coming from will allow you focus on those types of sources when you increase your referral sites. They also allow you to gain a better understanding of your online market – and target audience.

Bounce Rate

The bounce rate is the number of people who visit the homepage of your website, but do not visit other pages. If you have a high bounce rate, you either have all the necessary information on your homepage, or you are not giving your customers a reason to click further.

In Google Analytics, view the 'content' or 'pages' report and view the column stating bounce rate.

Errors

It is very important to track the errors that visitors receive while trying to access or view your website. For example, if someone links to your website, but makes a spelling error in typing the link, your users will see an error page in their browser, and will not ultimately make it to your website.

You can also receive reports on errors that customer's make when trying to type in your website address in their browser. You may wish to buy the domains with common spelling mistakes, and link those addresses to you true homepage. This will increase overall traffic and potential conversions.

Onsite Search Terms

If you have a 'search website' function on your website, it is useful to monitor which terms users are most frequently searching. This can provide valuable insight into the user friendliness of your site and your website's navigation system. This information will be included in the traffic reporting tool.

Bailout Rates

If you provide users with the option to purchase something on your website (i.e. shopping cart), then you can track where along the purchasing process people decided not to go through with the sale.

This could be at the first step of receiving the order summary and total, or further when stating shipping options. By obtaining this information, a company can reorganize or revamp their website to make the sales process more fluid and possibly encourage more purchases.

Here are the three main questions you should be asking yourself when evaluating your website presence:

- Who visits my website?
- Where do visitors come from?
- Which pages are viewed?

4

How to Profit from Direct Mail

Every time you mail an existing or potential customer a letter and ask them to respond or take action, you are running a direct-mail campaign.

Direct mail is a marketing strategy that can help you achieve a number of business objectives. From lead generation to customer retention, direct mail campaigns are a highly versatile and relatively cost-effective choice for business promotion.

What you probably don't realize is that direct mail is one of the most targeted marketing strategies you can implement, and one of the easiest to track, measure and analyze results.

It is also one of the most personal. Instead of an advertisement, flyer, newspaper insert or catalogue, you are sending each customer a personalized letter that is tailored to their unique needs and desires.

Getting the most out of your direct mail campaign is easy. With a laser-sharp mailing list and irresistible offer, your direct mail campaign can easily flood your business with qualified leads.

Let's get started!

A List of Ideal Customers

Unless you spend time carefully crafting a mailing list of ideal customers, you may as well pack and up go home. The success of a direct mail campaign largely rests on the pinpoint accuracy of your mailing list.

The only people you want on your list are your potential "ideal customers." The people who are most likely to buy from you – often and in large volumes – and who are a delight to deal with. They are the type of people who will account for 80% of your revenue, and just 20% of your total customer base.

You have a number of options when you are creating your mailing list:

- **Existing customer database**. This is a list of all of the people who have previously purchased from you. It is important to gather their full contact information at the time of sale so you will be able to get contact them again.

- **Existing leads database**. This is a list of all of the leads that have come through your door, but have not purchased from you. This may include those who responded to your last direct mail campaign, but have not yet become customers.

- **Outsourced list**. This is a list that has been purchased from a market research firm, the government, or the post office. These lists are pulled based on demographic information – age, sex, location, income, family structure, etc.

Putting the mailing list together

Once you have determined the source(s) for your mailing list, you will have to spend some time assembling it and preparing it for your mailing.

1. **Make sure all contacts are up to date.** Phone old contacts to confirm their mailing address. An out-of-date list will cost you money in printing and postage.

2. **Ensure all contacts are accurate to the list criteria.** Take a read through your list to make sure there are no contacts that shouldn't be on the list.

3. **Use a database management program to manage your mailing.** This will allow you to keep a master list, and create custom lists for each mailing. Remember to save the file name as something that describes the mailing so you can easily find it.

Writing Effective Direct Mail Pieces

Now that you have a laser-sharp mailing list, you will want to do everything you can to target your message to the recipients on your list.

An effective direct mail piece:

- **Has a clear structure.** The piece is clearly a letter – there is an engaging headline, clear message, point form list of benefits, and postscript.

- **Features an irresistible offer.** The purchase opportunity is too good for the target audience to refuse. It includes an element of scarcity and urgency.

- **Focuses on customer benefits.** The customer clearly understands "what's in it for me?" The product or service is clearly positioned as something of value and a solution to a need, problem, or desire.

- **Is personal and conversational.** The letter is personally addressed, and reads as though it was composed specifically for the recipient. It is written in conversational tone, with short sentences and limited description.

- **Is short.** The letter communicates what it needs to, and closes. It does not go on for pages in length. The messages are clear, succinct, and simple.

- **Is urgent.** The piece gives the reader to act immediately. There is a time limit or a quantity limit to the offer that requires an urgent response.

- **Includes a Postscript.** The offer or urgency is repeated after the signature at the bottom of the letter. Like a headline, everyone will read the P.S.

The Five-Step Direct Mail Campaign

1. Determine Your Target Audience

As we discussed above, you will want to ensure that you have the most accurate, targeted list possible for your direct mail campaign.

Be clear about the purpose for your direct mail campaign – this will help you decide if you want to send your letters to your entire target market, a segment of that market, existing customers, or potentially a referring business's customers. Then you can determine how you craft your offer, how you structure your letter, and when you choose to send it.

2. Choose what you want to say

What is the message you want to communicate to your target list? What can you offer them that will entice them to act immediately?

Create a specific offer for each direct mail campaign to ensure each time you communicate with your target list you have something new to say. Tailor this offer to each mailing list.

Decide what product or service benefits will be most compelling to your target audience, and include those benefits prominently in your letter.

3. Develop a compelling direct mail piece

You are in control of how your format your message. Are you sending a letter? A brochure and a letter? A postcard? The format of your direct mail piece needs to be tailored to your target list, and reflect your product or service. A younger audience may respond to a postcard, but an older audience may appreciate a formalized letter.

Ensure that whatever format you choose, the piece is professionally designed, prominently includes your logo and company branding, and is professionally produced.

This piece of paper has to act as an ambassador of your company – you absolutely need it to appear impressive and professional.

4. Pick your timing

Some products and purchase decisions are best made at certain times of the year, or the month. If your business or service is seasonal, then there are good times and bad times to try to generate leads. Consider the best purchase windows for the people in your target marketing. When do they get paid? When do they have the money to spend on your product/service? When do they spend the most money?

Anticipate these windows, and time your direct mail campaign accordingly. If you run a lawn sprinkler installation system and summer is your peak season, run a direct mail campaign mid-way through spring, and at the beginning of summer.

Some common time windows include:

- Holiday season (November – December)
- Fridays (paydays)
- The 15th and 30th of every months (also paydays)
- Seasons (Spring, Summer, Fall, Winter)
- Financial cycles (year-end, tax time)
- Sports seasons (hockey, football, baseball, etc.)

5. Follow up

Comprehensive follow up to a direct mail campaign means two things:

1. Following up on your letter with a phone call or second letter

Often it takes more than a letter to get a potential customer to take action. This can be a result of the accuracy of your mailing list, your offer, the time of the year, or the quality of the marketing material (brochure). If you are certain that your mailing list is accurate and up to date, follow up to the piece with a phone call, or send another letter.

2. Recording, measuring and analyzing your results.

It is essential that you evaluate each direct mail campaign based on your time and financial investment and your rate of response. How else will you be able to tell if it was a successful or effective strategy?

For each campaign, record and analyze the following information:

- Number of letters sent
- Number or responses as a percentage
- Number of sales directly resulting from the campaign
- Number of enquiries
- Total value of sales directly resulting from the campaign

Based on this information, determine if the campaign was successful (did it make you money?) or not. Consider making some changes to your list, your offer, or the piece itself, and try again.

5

How to Use Advertising for Immediate Profits

Why do you advertise?

Seems like a silly question, doesn't it? Placing ads in newspapers and on the radio seems like a no-brainer way of growing or maintaining your business. You let a group of people know where your business is and what you sell, and you'll always have customers dropping by, right?

Sure, it's a little more complicated than that. There's your powerful offer, your strong guarantee, the placement of your headline, and how you structure your body copy.

But what I'm really trying to drill down to is *why* you chose to place *that* ad. What is the specific purpose for each advertisement you send out into the world?

Without a solid purpose – or strategy – behind each and every advertisement, it is impossible to measure what is and is not working. If you placed an ad offering 2 for 1 shampoo one week, and sales for conditioner skyrocketed, would you consider your ad successful? Absolutely not. Sales might have gone up, but the reason you placed the ad was to speed sales on shampoo, which didn't happen.

The point is that each and every advertising dollar should be spent with purpose, focused on a desired outcome and relevant to the big picture. Advertising is expensive! What's the point, unless you're making your money back and then some?

Types of Advertising

There are endless options when it comes to choosing which media to place your advertisements with. The media is a broad and complicated industry, with highly segmented readership.

This can help and hurt your advertising efforts. You have access to highly targeted audiences, but you also may spend a great deal of money on expensive advertising that your target market doesn't go near.

Here are the major types of media advertising:

Print

Print is the most common form of advertising. Ad production is relatively easy and straightforward, and placement is less expensive than broadcast advertising. We'll be focusing on this form of advertising in detail later in the chapter.

Types of print media:
Newspapers – daily and weekly
Magazines
Trade Journals
Newsletters

Radio

Radio advertising reaches a broad audience within a geographic area. This form of advertising can be highly profitable for some businesses, and utterly useless for others. Always consider if there is a simpler, cheaper way of getting your message to your target audience.

Key points to consider for radio advertising:

Use of sounds, voices, tones
Length
Gaining listener's attention
Call to action

Television

Television advertising is largely out of reach for most small business budgets. Creating, developing, and producing TV spots is a costly endeavor, and does not always generate an acceptable return on investment.

This form of advertising generally reaches a broad audience, depending on the timeslot the ad spot airs. Typically, the most expensive airspace is during the region's most popular 6 o'clock news program, or prime time (6pm to 10pm) television line-up.

There are some cost-effective alternatives to TV advertising that you can implement online. You could create a promotional video for your company, and post it on your website and YouTube, or Facebook, or play it in your store. Be creative with your ad budget when it comes to broadcast media.

Online

Online advertising has emerged as an effective tool for your marketing efforts. Internet usage has dramatically increased, and usage patterns have become easier to identify. This form of advertising also allows you to reach a highly qualified audience with minimal investment in ad creation.

Places to advertise online:

>Facebook
>Google Adwords
>Online media (online newspapers and broadcast stations)
>Craigslist
>Banner ads on complementary websites

Classified

Classified advertising is one of the most highly targeted and cost-effective choices you can make in your overall strategy. People who read classifieds have typically made a decision to buy something, and are looking for places to do so. This is also a great way to test your headlines, offer, and guarantee before you invest in higher-priced advertising.

Classified ad types:

>Daily and weekly newspapers
>Online
>Trade journals

Specific tips for effective classified ads:

- Pick a format for your ad within the specifications of the publication. Will it look like a print display ad? A semi-display ad? A classic line ad? This will affect how you structure your message.

- Choose the category – or two – that best fit with what you have to offer. If two apply, place an ad in both and measure which category generated more leads.

- Grab the attention of your reader with a killer headline, then list benefits, make an irresistible offer, and offer a strong guarantee. Keep the layout simple and ensure the font size is easy to read.

- Notice how other companies are creating their ads, and do something to stand out. The classifieds page is typically cluttered and full of text, so you will need to distinguish your business in some way.

- Use standard abbreviations when creating line ads to maintain consistency. Ask the ad department for a list of abbreviations they typically use.

Niche

Niche advertising can take any of the forms discussed above. The advantage of niche advertising is the super segmentation of each outlet's audience. Typically, there is a very small market in each niche, and a single publication that caters to it. This is very effective for companies who have no need for broad market advertising in traditional or mainstream publications.

Types of niche advertising:

    Trade journals
    Alternative media
    Online blogs
    Internal communications – newsletters, etc.

Your Advertising Strategy

Develop a strategy that is purpose driven.

Know exactly why you are choosing advertising, as well as the objective of each and every ad. Compare the benefits of advertising to other promotional strategies like media relations, direct mail, referral strategies and customer loyalty programs.

Some common objectives for advertising strategies include:

- Generate qualified leads
- Increase sales
- Promote new products or services
- Position products or services
- Increase business awareness
- Maintain business awareness
- Complement existing promotional strategies

These objectives will dictate where you advertise, how big each of your advertisements is, and how often you advertise in each outlet.

Find your target audience.

Before you do *anything*, get a solid handle on who your target market is, and each of the segments within it. Think about demographic factors like age, sex, location and occupation, as well as behavioral factors like spending motivations and habits.

The composition of your target audience will be the deciding factor when choosing which media to advertise with, and what to say in each of the advertisements.

Decide on a frequency.

The frequency of your advertising campaign will depend on a number of factors, including budget, purpose, outlet, results, and timing. You may wish to publish a weekly ad that includes a coupon in your local paper. Or, you may only need to advertise a few times a year, just before your peak seasons.

Establish an advertising schedule for the year, or at least each quarter, and plan each advertisement in advance. This will ensure you are not scrambling to place an ad at the last minute, and that each ad is part of an overall proactive strategy instead of a reactive one.

Choose your outlets.

Decide where you are going to advertise and how often in each outlet. You may wish to choose a variety of media to reach several target audiences, or just a large daily newspaper where the most number of people will see it.

It is a good idea when you are starting a new campaign to test its effectiveness in smaller, less expensive publications. Based on the results, you can make changes to the ad and place it in the more expensive outlets.

Remember that although budget is a large factor when deciding on advertising mediums, it is entirely possible to implement a successful ad campaign with minimal cost investment. The key is to make sure that each dollar you spend is carefully thought through – and that your ads are placed in publications that will reach your ideal customers.

Maximize your ad spend with bulk purchases.

If you plan to advertise in a specific publication several times in a given time period, you will benefit from a meeting with the sales representative to review your needs. Often, media outlets will offer discounted rates for multiple placements.

Remember that one company may own several media outlets – including TV, radio, and online media. Ask your sales rep for other discount opportunities when advertising within the ownership group.

Remember to test and measure

How will you know if your campaign is successful if you don't test and measure the results? The only true mistake you can make in advertising is neglecting to track and analyze the results each ad generates.

Get in the habit of keeping a copy of each ad, and record all the details of the placement, including publication, cost, date, response rate, and conversion rate. Many publications will mail you a clipping of your advertisement with your account statement, but don't rely on this as a clipping service.

Evaluate the effectiveness of each ad you place, and learn from what isn't working. If you are advertising in several outlets, make sure asking customers where they saw your ad is part of your incoming phone script and sales script. You will need to monitor not only what types of ads work the best, but also where the ads generate the highest response.

Creating Your Advertisement

You don't need to rely on professional copywriting or design assistance when crafting advertisements from your business. Spend your time and resources on what you are saying, ensure the 'how you say it' is clear, clean, and easy to read.

Ad copy

    Headlines
- Take at least half of the time you spend creating your ad, and focus on the headline. Your headline will be the difference between your ad getting read – or not. Boldface your headlines for impact.

- You have about five seconds to grab the reader's attention, so create a headline that sparks curiosity, communicates benefits, or states something unbelievable.

Sub Headlines

- The purpose of your sub headline is to elaborate on your headline, and convince the audience to read the body copy. All the rules of headline writing apply. If you did not mention benefits in your headline, do it in your sub headline. Clearly tell the reader what is "in it for them," and get them reading on.

Body Copy

- Choose your words wisely – you don't have room for lengthy paragraphs. Use bullet points to convey benefits wherever possible, and keep your sentences short. You typically only have about 45 words to convince the customer to keep reading.

- Remember to always include your contact information – phone number and website address at the very least. This seems obvious, but can be forgotten in the design process.

Ad Layout

Size

- Choose your ad size based on the purpose of the ad, and the budget you have available. Larger ads are more expensive, but you do need enough space to communicate your key messages to the audience.

- If you place regular ads to maintain a presence in the local paper, you likely don't need full pages of space. Alternately, if you are launching a new product or service, or having a blowout sale, you will want to buy more space to increase the potential impact.

Graphics

- Graphics should comprise about 25% of your total ad space, and more if you have a small amount of copy. Avoid drawings and clip art. Photographs will generate a better response. Don't underestimate the importance of white space. Give the reader space to "rest" their eyes between headlines and body copy paragraphs.

Font

- Choose clean fonts that are easy to read. Times New Roman and Arial are effective, simple choices. If you use two fonts in your advertisement, make sure you do not combine serif and sans serif fonts, and you keep consistency amongst headers and body copy.

- Ensure that none of your copy is smaller than 9pt. Your audience won't take the time or spend the effort to read tiny copy.

6

Systemizing Your Business and Developing Effective Processes

One of the biggest mistakes a business owner can make is to create a company that is dependent on the owner's involvement for the success of its daily operations. This is called working "in" your business. You're writing basic sales letters, licking stamps, and guiding staff step-by-step through each task.

There are a number of problems with this approach. One is redundancy. You're paying your staff to carry out tasks that you eventually complete. The second is poor time management. You're spending your day – at your high hourly rate – on tasks as they arise, leaving little room for the tasks you need to be focused on.

However, the biggest issue I have with this approach is that countless intelligent business owners are spending the majority of their time operating their business, instead of *growing* it.

A good test of this is to ask yourself, what would happen if you took off to a hot sunny destination for three weeks and left your cell phone, PDA and laptop at home. Would your business be able to continue operating?

If you said no, then this chapter is for you.

Systemizing your business is about putting policies and procedures in place to make your business operations run smoother – and more importantly – without your constant involvement. With your newfound free time, **you will be able to focus your efforts on the bigger picture: strategically growing your business.**

Why Systemize?

For most small business owners, systems simply mean freedom from the day-to-day functioning of their organization. The company runs smoothly, makes a profit, and provides a high level of service – regardless of the owner's involvement.

Systemizing your business is also a healthy way to plan for the future. You're not going to be working forever – what happens when you retire? How will you transition your business to new ownership or management? How will you take that vacation you've been dreaming of?

Businesses that function without their ownership are also highly valuable to investors. Systemizing your business can position it in a favorable light for purchase, and merit a high price tag.

A system is any process, policy, or procedure that consistently achieves the same result, regardless of who is completing the task.

Any task that is performed in your business more than once can be systemized. Ideally, the tasks that are completed on a cyclical basis – daily, weekly, monthly, and quarterly – should be systemized so much so that anyone can perform them.

Systems can take many forms – from manuals and instruction sheets, to signs, banners, and audio or video recordings. They don't have to be elaborate or extensive, just provide enough information in step-by-step form to guide the person performing the task.

Benefits of Business Systems

There are unlimited benefits available to you and your business through systemization. The more systems you can successfully implement, the more benefits you'll see.

- Better cost management
- Improved time management
- Clearer expectations of staff
- More effective staff training and orientation
- Increased productivity (and potentially profits)
- Happier customers (consistent service)
- Maximized conversion rates
- Increased staff respect for your time
- Increased level of individual initiative
- Greater focus on long-term business growth

Taking Stock of Your Existing Systems

The first step in systemizing your business is taking a long look at the existing systems (if any) in your business. At this point, you can look for any systems that have simply emerged as "the way we do things here."

How do your staff answer the phone? What is the process customers go through when dealing with your business? How are employees hired? Trained? How is performance Reviewed and rewarded?

Some of your systems may be highly effective, and not require any changes. Others may be ineffective and require some reworking. If you have previously established some systems, now is a good time to check-in and evaluate how well they are functioning.

Use the following chart to record what systems currently exist in your business.

Existing Systems	
Administration	
Financials	

Communication	
Customer Relations	
Employees	
Marketing	
Data	

Seven Areas to Systemize

There is no doubt that system creation – especially when none exist to begin with – is a daunting and time-consuming task. For many businesses, it can be difficult to determine where to start to make the best use of their time from the onset.

Here are seven main areas of your business you can to systemize. Begin with one area, and move to the other areas as you are ready.

Alternately, start with one or two systems within each area, and evaluate how those new systems affect your business. Each business will require its own unique set of systems.

1. Administration

This is an important area of your business to systemize because administrative roles tend to see a high turnover. A series of systems will reduce training time, and keep you from explaining how the phones are to be answered each time a new receptionist joins your team.

Administrative Systems	
Opening and closing procedures	Filing and paper management
Phone greeting	Workflow
Mail processing	Document production
Sending couriers	Inventory management
Office maintenance (watering plants, emptying recycle bins, etc.)	Order processing
	Making orders

2. Financials

This is one area of systems that you will need to keep a close eye on – but that doesn't mean you have to do the work yourself. Financial management systems are everything from tracking credit card purchases to invoicing clients and following up on overdue accounts.

These systems will help to prevent employee theft, and allow you to always have a clear picture of your numbers. It will allow you to control purchasing, and ensure that each decision is signed-off on.

Financial Systems	
Purchasing	Profit / loss statements
Credit card purchase tracking	Invoicing
Accounts payable	Daily cash out
Accounts receivable	Petty cash
Bank deposits	Employee expenses
Cutting checks	Payroll
Tax payments	Commission payments

3. Communications

The area of communication is essential and time consuming for any business. Fax cover letters, sales letters, internal memos, reports, and newsletters are items that need to be created regularly by different people in your organization.

Most of the time, these communications aren't much different from one to the next, yet each are created from scratch by a different person. There is a huge opportunity for systemization in this area of your business. Systemized communication ensures consistency and company differentiation.

Communication Systems	
Internal memo template	Newsletter template
Fax cover template	Sales letter template(s)

Letterhead template	Meeting minutes template
Team meeting agenda	Report template
Sending faxes	Internal meetings
Internal emails	Scheduling

4. Customer Relations

Another important area for systemization is customer relations. This includes everything the customer sees or touches in your company, as well as any interaction they might have with you or your staff members.

Establishing a customer relations system will also ensure that new staff members understand how customers are handled in *your* business. It will allow you to maintain a high level of customer service, without constantly reminding staff of your policies. It will also ensure that the success of your customer relations and retention does not hinge on you or any other individual salesperson.

Customer Relations Systems	
Incoming phone call script	Sales process
Outgoing phone call script	Sales script
Customer service standards	Newsletter templates
Customer retention strategy	Ongoing customer communication strategy
Customer communications templates	Customer liaison policy

5. Employees

Create systems in your business for hiring, training, and developing your employees. This will establish clear expectations for the employee, and streamline time consuming activities like recruitment.

Employees with clear expectations who work within clear structures are happier and more productive. They are motivated to achieve 'A' when they know they will receive 'B' if they do. Establishing a clear training manual will also save you and your staff the time and hassle of training each new staff member on the fly.

Employee Systems	
Employee recruitment	Staff uniforms or dress code
Employee retention	Employee training
Incentive and rewards program	Ongoing training and professional development
Regular employee reviews	
Employee feedback structure	Job descriptions and role profiles

6. Marketing

This is likely an area in which you spend a large part of your time. You focus on generating new leads and getting more people to call you or walk through your doors. These efforts can be systemized and delegated to other staff members.

Use the information in this program to create simple systems for your basic promotional efforts. Any one of your staff should be able to pick up a marketing manual and implement a successful direct mail campaign or place a purposeful advertisement.

Marketing Systems	
Referral program	Regular advertisements
Customer retention program	Advertisement creation system
Regular promotions	Direct mail system
Marketing calendar	Sales procedures
Enquiries management	Lead management

7. Data

While we like to think we operate a paperless office, often the opposite is true. Your business needs to have clear systems for managing paper and electronic information to ensure that information is protected, easily accessed, and only kept when necessary.

Data management systems help you keep your office organized. Everyone knows where information is to be stored, and how it is to be handled, which prevents big stacks of paper with no place to go.

Ensure that within your data management systems you include a data backup system. That way, if anything happens to you server or computer software, your data – and potentially your business – is protected.

Data Management Systems	
IT Management	Client file system
Data backup	Project file system

Computer repairs Electronic information storage	Point of sale system Financial data management

Implementing New Systems

If you completed the exercise earlier in this chapter, you will have a good idea of the systems that are currently in place in your business. The next step is to determine what systems you need to create in your business.

To do this you will need to get a better understanding of the tasks that you and your employees complete on a daily and weekly basis. If you operate a timesheet program, this can be a good source of information. Alternately, ask staff to keep a daily log for a week of all the tasks they contribute to or complete. Doing so will not only give you valuable insight into their how they spend their time on a daily basis, but also involve them in the systemizing process.

Review all task logs or timesheet records at the end of the week, remove duplicates, and group like tasks together. From here you can categorize the tasks into business areas like the seven listed above, or create your own categories.

Then, you will need to prioritize and plan your system creation and implementation efforts. Choose one from each category, or one category to focus on at a time. The amount you can take on will depend on your business needs, and the staff resources you have available to you for this process.

Remember that system creation is a long-term process – not something that will transform your business overnight. Be patient, and focus on the items that hold the highest priority.

Creating Your Systems

There is a big variety of ways you can create systems for your business – depending on the type of system you need and the type of business you operate. Some systems will be short and simple – i.e., a laminated sign in the kitchen that outlines step-by-step how to make the coffee – while others will be more complex – i.e., your sales scripts or letter templates.

One thing all of your systems have in common is steps. There is a linear process involved from start to finish. Begin by writing out each of the steps involved in completing the task, and provide as much detail as you can.

Then, review your step-by-step guide with the employee(s) who regularly complete the task and gather their feedback. Once you have incorporated their input, decide what format the system needs to be in: manual, laminated instruction sheet, sign, office memo, etc.

Testing Your Systems

Now that you have created a system, you will need to make sure that it works. More specifically, you need to make sure that it works without your involvement.

Implement the new system for an appropriate period of time – a week or month – then ask for input from staff, suppliers and vendors, and customers. Evaluate if it is informative enough for your staff, seamless enough for your suppliers, and whether or not it meets or exceeds your customer's needs.

Take that feedback and revise the system accordingly. You will rarely get the system right the first time – so be patient.

Systems will also need to be evaluated and revised on a regular basis to ensure your business processes are kept up to date. Structure an annual or bi-annual review of systems, and stick to it.

Employee Buy-In

It will be nearly impossible for you to develop effective systems without the involvement and input of your employees. These are the people who will be using the systems, and who are completing the tasks on a regular basis without systems. They have a wealth of knowledge to assist you in this process.

Employees can also draft the systems for you to review and finalize. This will make the systemization process a much faster and more efficient one.

It is also important to note that when you introduce new systems into your company, there may be a natural resistance to the change. People –

including your employees – are habitual people who can become set in the way they are used to doing things.

Delegation

The final step to systemizing your business is delegation. What is the point of creating systems unless someone other than you can use them to perform tasks?

This doesn't have to mean completely removing your involvement from the process, but it does mean giving your employees enough freedom to complete the task within the structure of the systems you have spent time and considerable thought creating.

After that, allow yourself the freedom of focusing on the tasks that you most enjoy, and most deserve your time – like creating big picture strategies to grow your business and increase your profits.

7

Generating an Unlimited Amount of Leads for Your Business

Where do your customers come from?

Most people would probably choose advertising as an answer. Or referrals. Or direct mail campaigns. This may seem true, but it's not really accurate.

Your customers come from leads that have been turned into sales. Each customer goes through a two-step process before they arrive with their wallets open. They have been converted from a member of a target market, to a lead, then to a customer.

So, would it not stand to reason then, that when you advertise or send any marketing material out to your target market, that you're not really trying to generate customers? That instead, you're trying to generate leads.

When you look at your marketing campaign from this perspective, the idea of generating leads as compared to customers seems a lot less daunting. The pressure of closing sales is no longer placed on advertisements or brochures.

From this perspective, the **general purpose of your advertising and marketing efforts is then to generate leads from qualified customers.** Seems easy enough, doesn't it?

Where Are Your Leads Coming From?

If I asked you to tell me the top three ways you generate new sales leads, what would you say?

- Advertising?
- Word of mouth?
- Networking?
- …don't know?

The first step toward increasing your leads is in understanding how many leads you currently get on a regular basis, as well as where they come from. Otherwise, how will you know when you're getting more phone calls or walk-in customers?

If you don't know where your leads come from, start *today*. Start asking every customer that comes through your door, "how did you hear about us?" or "what brought you in today?" Ask every customer that calls where they found your telephone number, or email address. Then, *record the information for at least an entire week.*

When you're finished, take a look at your spreadsheet and write your top three lead generators here:

1. _____

2. _____

3. _____

From Lead to Customer: Conversion Rates

Leads mean nothing to your business unless you convert them into customers. You could get hundreds of leads from a single advertisement, but unless those leads result in purchases, it's been a largely unsuccessful (and costly) campaign.

The ratio of leads (potential customers) to transactions (actual customers) is called your conversion rate. Simply divide the number of customers who actually purchased something by the number of customers who inquired about your product or service, and multiply by 100.

 # transactions / # leads x 100 = % conversion rate

If, in a given week, I have 879 customers come into my store, and 143 of them purchase something, the formula would look like this:

[143 (customers) / 879 (leads)] x 100 = 16.25% conversion rate

What's Your Conversion Rate?

Based on the formula above, you can see that the higher your conversion rate, the more profitable the business.

Your next step is to determine you own current conversion rate. Add up the number of leads you sourced in the last section, and divide that number into the total transactions that took place in the same week.

Write your conversion rate here:
_____.

Quality (or Qualified) Leads

Based on our review of conversion rates, we can see that the number of leads you generate means nothing unless those leads are being converted into customers.

So what affects your ability (and the ability of your team) to turn leads into customers? Do you need to improve your scripts? Your product or service? Find a more competitive edge in the marketplace?

Maybe. But the first step toward increasing conversion rates is to evaluate the leads you are currently generating, and make sure those leads are the right ones.

What are Quality Leads?

Potential customers are potential customers, right? Anyone who walks into your store or picks up the phone to call your business could be convinced to purchase from you, right? Not necessarily, but this is a common assumption most business owners make.

Quality leads are the people who are the most likely to buy your product or service. They are the qualified buyers who comprise your target market. Anyone might walk in off the street to browse a furniture store – regardless of whether or not they are in the market for a new couch or bed frame. This lead is solely interested in browsing, and is not likely to be converted to a customer.

A quality lead would be someone looking for a new kitchen table, and who specifically drove to that same furniture because a friend had raved about the service they received that month. **These are the kinds of leads you need to focus on generating.**

How Do You Get Quality Leads?

- **Know your target market**. Get a handle on who your customers are – the people who are most likely to buy your product or service. Know their age, sex, income, and purchase motivations. From that information you can determine how best to reach your specific audience.

- **Focus on the 80/20 rule.** A common statistic in business is that 80% of your revenue comes from 20% of your customers. These are your star clients, or your ideal clients. These are the clients you should focus your efforts on recruiting. This is the easiest way to grow your business and your income.

- **Get specific.** Focus not only on who you want to attract, but how you're going to attract them. If you're trying to generate leads from a specific market segment, craft a unique offer to get their attention.

- **Be proactive.** Once you've generated a slew of leads, make sure you have the resources to follow up on them. Be diligent and aggressive, and follow up in a timely manner. You've done to work to get them, now reel them in.

Get More Leads from Your Existing Strategies

Increasing your lead generation doesn't necessarily mean diving in and implementing an expensive array of new marketing strategies. Marketing and customer outreach for the purpose of lead generation can be inexpensive, and bring a high return on investment.

You are likely already implementing many of these strategies. With a little tweaking or refinement, you can easily double your leads, and ensure they are more qualified.

Here are some popular ways to generate quality leads:

Direct Mail to Your Ideal Customers

Direct mail is one of the fastest and most effective ways to generate leads that will build your business. It's a simple strategy – in fact, you're probably already reaching out to potential clients through direct mail letters with enticing offers.

The secret to doubling your results is to craft your direct mail campaigns specifically for a highly targeted audience of your *ideal* customers.

Your ideal customers are the people who will buy the most of your products or services. They are the customers who will buy from you over and over again, and refer your business to their friends. They are the group of 20% of your clients who make up 80% of your revenue.

Identify your ideal customers

Who are your ideal customers? What is their age, sex, income, location and purchase motivation? Where do they live? How do they spend their money? Be as specific as possible.

Once you have identified who your ideal customers are, you can begin to determine how you can go about reaching them. Will you mail to households or apartment buildings? Families or retirees? Direct mail lists are available for purchase from a wide range of companies, and can be segregated into a variety of demographic and sociographic categories.

Craft a special offer

Create an offer that's too good to refuse – not for your entire target market, but for your ideal customer. How can you cater to their unique needs and wants? What will be irresistible for them?

For example, if you operate a furniture store, your target market is a broad range of people. However, if you are targeting young families, your offer will be much different than one you may craft for empty-nesters.

Court them for their business

Don't stop at a single mail-out. Sometimes people will throw your letter away two or three times before they are motivated to act. Treat your direct mail campaign like a courtship, and understand that it will happen over time.

First send a letter introducing yourself, and your irresistible offer. Then follow up on a monthly basis with additional letters, newsletters, offers, or flyers. Repetition and reinforcement of your presence is how your customer will go from saying, "who is this company" to "I buy from this company."

Advertise for lead generation

Statistics show that nearly 50% of all purchase decisions are motivated by advertising. It can also be a relatively cost effective way of generating leads.

We've already discussed the importance of ensuring your advertisements are purpose-focused. The general purpose of most advertisements is to increase sales – which starts with leads. However ads that are created solely for lead generation – that is, to get the customers to pick up the phone or walk in the store – are a category of their own.

Lead generation ads are simply designed and create a sense of curiosity or mystery. Often, they feature an almost unbelievable offer. Their purpose is not to convince the customer to buy, but to contact the business for more information.

As always, when you are targeting your ideal audience, you'll need to ensure that your ads are placed prominently in publications that audience reads. This doesn't mean you have to fork over the cash for expensive display ads. Inexpensive advertising in e-mail newsletters, classifieds, and the yellow pages are very effective for lead generation.

Here are some tips for lead generation advertising:

Leverage low-cost advertising

Place ads in the yellow pages, classifieds section, e-mail newsletters, and online. If your target audience is technology savvy, consider new forms of advertising like Facebook and Google Adwords.

Spark curiosity

Don't give them all the information they need to make a decision. Ask them to contact you for the full story, or the complete details of the seemingly outrageous offer.

Grab them with a killer headline

Like all advertising, a compelling headline is essential. Focus on the greatest benefits to the customer, or feature an unbelievable offer.

Referrals and host beneficiary relationships

A referral system is one of the most profitable systems you can create in your business. The beauty is once it's set up, it often runs itself.

Customers that come to you through referrals are often your "ideal customers." They are already trusting and willing to buy. This is one of the most cost-effective methods of generating new business, and is often the most profitable. These referral clients will buy more, faster, and refer further business to your company.

Referrals naturally happen without much effort for reputable businesses, but with a proactive referral strategy you'll certainly double or triple your referrals. Sometimes, you just need to ask!

Here are some easy strategies you can begin to implement today:

Referral incentives

Give your customers a reason to refer business to you. Reward them with discounts, gifts, or free service in exchange for a successful referral.

Referral program

Offer new customers a free product or service to get them in the door. Then, at the end of the transaction, give them three more 'coupons' for the same free product or service that they can give to their friends. Do the same with their friends. This ongoing program will bring you more business than you can imagine.

Host-beneficiary relationships

Forge alliances with non-competitive companies who target your ideal customers. Create cross-promotion and cross-referral direct mail campaigns that benefit both businesses.

Lead Management Systems

Once your lead generation strategies are in place, you'll also need a system to manage incoming inquiries. You'll need to ensure you receive enough information from each lead to follow up on at a later date. You'll also need to create a system to organize that information, and track the lead as it is converted into a sale.

Gathering Information from Your Leads

Here is a list of information you should gather from your leads. This list can be customized to the needs of your business, and the type of information you can realistically ask for from your potential customers.

- Company Name
- Name of Contact
- Alternate Contact Person
- Mailing Address
- Phone Number
- Fax Number
- Cell Phone
- Email Address
- Website Address
- Product of Interest
- Other Competitors Engage

Lead List Management Methods:

Once you have gathered information from your lead, you'll need a system to organize their information and keep a detailed contact history.

The simplest way to do this is with a database program, but you can also use a variety of hard copy methods.

Electronic Database Programs

- High level of organization available
- Unlimited space for notes and record-keeping
- Data-entry required
- Examples include: MS Outlook, MS Excel, Maximizer
- Customer Relationship Management Software

Index Cards

- Variety of sizes: 3x5, 4X6 or 5X8
- Basic contact information on one side
- Notes on the other side
- Easy to organize and sort

Rolodex System

- Maintain more contacts than index card system
- Easily organized and compact
- Basic contact information on one side
- Notes on the other side
- Can keep phone conversation and purchase details

Notebook

- Best if leads are managed by a single person
- Lots of room for notes
- Inexpensive
- Difficult to re-organize
- Best for smaller lists

Business Card Organizer

- Best for small lists – under 100
- Limited space for notes
- No data entry required
- Rolodex-style, or clear binder pages

To learn the 3 biggest mistakes all business owners make and how to avoid them, visit www.resultsorientedcoaching.com

8

Use Goal Setting Effectively

We've all heard about the power of setting goals. Everyone has surely seen statistics that connect goal setting to success in both your business life, and your personal life. I'm sure if I asked you today what your goals are, you could rattle off a few wants and hopes without thinking too long.

However, what most people do not realize is that the power of goal setting lies in *writing goals down*. Committing goals to paper and reviewing them regularly gives you a 95% higher chance of achieving your desired outcomes. Studies have shown that only three to five percent of people in the world have written goals – the same three to five percent who have achieve success in business and earn considerable wealth.

These studies have also found that by retirement, only four per cent of people in the world will have enough accumulated wealth to maintain their income level, and quality of life. As a business owner, it is essential that you develop a plan for your retirement, but it is equally essential that you develop a plan for your success.

This chapter focuses on the power of goal setting as part of your business success. We'll teach you to set SMART goals that are rooted in your own personal value system, and supporting techniques to achieve your goals faster.

What are Goals?

Goals are clear targets that are attached to a specific time frame and action plan; they focus your efforts, and drive your motivation in a clear direction. Goals are different from dreams in that they outline a plan of action, while dreams are a conceptual vision of your wish or desired outcome.

Goals require work; work on yourself, work for your business, and work for others. You cannot achieve a goal – no matter how badly you want it – without being prepared to make a considerable effort. If you are ready to invest your time and energy, goals will help you to:

- Realize a dream or wish for your personal or business life
- Make a change in your life – add positive, or remove negative
- Improve your skills and performance ability
- Start or change a habit – positive or negative

Why Set Goals?

As we've already reviewed, setting goals and committing them to paper is the most effective way to cultivate success. The most important reason to set a goal is **to attach a clear action plan to a desired outcome.**

Goals help focus our time and energy on one (or several) key outcome at a time. Many business owners have hundreds of ideas whirring around in their heads at any one time, on top of daily responsibilities. By writing down and focusing on a few ideas at a time, you can prioritize and concentrate your efforts, avoid being stretched too thin, and produce greater results.

Since goals attach action to outcomes, goals can help to break down big dreams into manageable (and achievable) sections. Creating a multi-goal strategy will put a road map in place to help you get to your desired outcome. If your goal is to start a pizza business and make six figures a year, there are a number of smaller steps to achieve before you achieve your end result.

Success doesn't happen by itself. It is the result of consistent and committed action by an individual who is driven to achieve something. Success means something different for everyone, so creating goals is a personal endeavor. Goals can be large and small, personal and public, financial and spiritual. It is not the size of the goal that matters; what matters is that you write the goal down and commit to making the effort required to achieve it.

What happens when I achieve a goal?

You should congratulate yourself and your team, of course! By rewarding yourself and your team after every achievement, you not only train your mind to associate hard work with reward, but develop loyalty among your employees.

You should also ask yourself if your achievement can be taken to the next level, or if your goal can be stretched by building on the effort you have already made. Consistently setting new and higher targets will lay the framework for constant improvement and personal and professional growth.

Power of Positive Thinking

When was the last time you tuned into your internal stream of consciousness? What does the stream of thoughts that run through your mind sound like? Are they positive? Negative? Are they logical? Reasonable?

Positive thinking and healthy self-talk are the most important business tools you can ever cultivate; by programming a positive stream of subconscious thoughts into your mind, you can control your reality, and ultimately your goals. Think about someone you know who is constantly negative; someone who complains and whines and makes excuses for their unhappiness. How successful are they? How do their fears and doubts become reality in their world?

You are what you continuously believe about yourself and your environment. If you focus your mind on something in your mental world, it will nearly always manifest as reality in your physical world.

Positive thinking is a key part of setting goals. You won't achieve your goal until you believe that you can. You will achieve your goals faster when you believe in yourself, and the people around you who are helping to make your goal a reality.

Successful people are rooted in a strong belief system – belief in themselves, belief in the work they are doing, and belief in the people around them. They are motivated to improve and learn, but also confident in their existing skills and knowledge. Their positive attitude and energy is clearly felt in everything they do.

Ever notice how complainers usually surround themselves with other complainers? The same is true of positive thinkers. If you cultivate an upbeat and positive attitude, you will be surrounded by people who share your values and outlook on life.

Too often, people and our society subscribe to a continuous stream of negative chatter. The more you hear it, the more you'll believe it.

How many times have you heard:

- That's impossible.
- Don't even bother.
- It's already been done.
- We tried that, and it didn't work.
- You're too young.
- You're too old.
- You'll never get there.
- You'll never get that done.
- You can't do that.

Positive thinking and positive influences will provide the support you need to achieve your goals. Choose your friends and close colleagues wisely, and surround yourself with positive thinkers.

Creating SMART Goals

SMART goals are just that: smart. Whether you are setting goals for your personal life, your business, or with your employees, goals that have been developed with the SMART principle have a higher probability of being achieved.

The SMART Principle

1. Specific

Specific goals are clearer and easier to achieve than nonspecific goals. When writing down your goal, ask yourself the five "W" questions to narrow in on what exactly you are aiming for. Who? Where? What? When? Why?

For example, instead of a nonspecific goal like, "get in shape for the summer," a specific goal would be, "go to the gym three times a week and eat twice as many vegetables."

2. Measurable

If you can't measure your goal, how will you know when you've achieved it? Measurable goals help you clearly see where you are, and where you want to be. You can see change happen as it happens.

Measurable goals can also be broken down and managed in smaller pieces. They make it easier to create an action plan or identify the steps required to achieve your goal. You can track your progress, revise your plan, and celebrate each small achievement. For example, instead of aiming to increase revenue in 2009, you can set out to increase revenue by 30% in the next 12 months, and celebrate each 10% along the way.

3. Achievable

Goals that are achievable have a higher chance of being realized. While it is important to think big, and dream big, too often people set goals that are simply beyond their capabilities and wind up disappointed. Goals can stretch you, but they should always be feasible to maintain your motivation and commitment.

For example, if you want to complete your first triathlon but you've never run a mile in your life, you would be setting a goal that was beyond your current capabilities. If you decided instead to train for a five mile race in six months, you would be setting an achievable goal.

4. Relevant

Relevant – or realistic – goals are goals that have a logical place in your life or your overall business strategy. The goal's action plan can be reasonably integrated into your life, with a realistic amount of effort.

For example, if your goal is to train to climb to base camp at Mount Everest within one year and you're about to launch a start-up business, you may need to question the relevance of your goal in the context of your current commitments.

5. Timely

It is essential for every goal to be attached to a time-frame – otherwise it is merely a dream. Check in to make sure that your time-frame is realistic - not too short, or too long. This will keep you motivated and committed to your action plan, and allow you track your progress.

Autosuggestion + Visualization

Autosuggestion and visualization are two techniques that can assist you in achieving your goals. Some of the most well-known and successful people in the world use these techniques, and it is not coincidence that they are masters in their own fields of business and sport. A few of these people include:

- Michael Phelps (Olympic Swimmer)
- Andre Agassi (Tennis)

- Donald Trump (Real Estate)
- Wayne Gretzky (Hockey)
- Bill Gates (Microsoft)
- Walt Disney (Entertainment)

Of course, each of these people have a high degree of talent, ambition, intelligence and drive. However, to reach the top of their respective field, they have each used Autosuggestion and Visualization.

Autosuggestion

Autosuggestion is your internal dialogue; the constant stream of thoughts and comments that flows through your mind, and impacts what you think about yourself and how you perceive situations.

Since you were a small child, this self-talk has been influenced by your experiences and has programmed your mind to think and react in certain ways. The good news is that you can reprogram your mind and customize your self-talk any way you like. That is the power of Autosuggestion.

To begin practicing Autosuggestion, make sure you are relaxed and open to trying the technique; an ideal time is just before bed, or when you have some time to sit quietly. Then, repeat positive affirmations to yourself about the ideal outcome. Top sports and business people will often practice just before a big game or meeting.

Some examples of positive self-talk or autosuggestion include:

- I will lead my team to a victory tonight!
- I will be relaxed open to meeting new people at the party tonight!
- I will deliver a clear and impacting speech!
- I will stop worrying and tackle this problem tomorrow!
- I will stand up for my own ideas in the meeting!
- I will remember everything I have studied for the test tomorrow!

Visualization

Visualization is a practice complementary to Autosuggestion. While you can repeat affirmations to yourself over and over, combining this practice with visualization is twice as powerful.

Visualization is exactly what it sounds like: repeatedly visualizing how something is going to happen in your mind's eye. Nearly everyone in sports practices this technique. It has been proven to enhance performance better than practice alone.

This technique can easily be applied to business. For example, prior to any presentation or meeting where you must speak, present or "perform." You can also visualize yourself being incredibly productive and effective in your office. Or, having a discussion with your spouse calmly and rationally.

Elements to think about during visualization:

- What does the room look like?
- What do the people in the room look like?
- What is their mood? How do they receive me?
- What image do I project?
- How do I look?
- How do I behave? What is my attitude?
- What is the outcome?

9

How to Use Testimonials and Profit from Social Proof

The Power of Testimonials

Testimonials are simply the single most powerful asset you can have in your marketing toolkit. When your customers tell others about the benefits of choosing your business, it is a thousand times more powerful than the same words from your mouth.

The words and opinions of others motivate people to spend money every day. From celebrity endorsements on TV and in magazines, to casual conversations with friends, decisions about what product or service to buy – and what brand or provider – are heavily influenced by those who have purchased before.

Why? There are several reasons. Many people have an inherent distrust of salespeople, and a skepticism toward marketing materials. Others are bombarded with choice, and are looking for some sense of security in their purchase decision.

Testimonials build the credibility of your business, break down natural barriers, and create a sense of trust for the consumer. They have an incredible ability to persuade customers to buy, and to buy from you. Think about the last time someone recommended a brand of laundry detergent, a bottle of wine, or a plumber to you. Their positive experience had more of an impact on your decision to buy than any advertisement or discount.

When it comes to spending money, people want a sure bet. They want to know that someone else has bought before, and they want to know that the product or service has delivered the promised results. A testimonial for your business is worth more than any copywriter, clever ad slogan, or sales pitch.

Customers Who Give Testimonials

When people put their name and reputation on paper to endorse something, it creates a sense of loyalty; if questioned, they will back their decision, even if they find later their decision was wrong.

When someone is willing to endorse your product or service in writing, they have likely already started a word-of-mouth chain of verbal testimonials about their positive experience. Remember the last time you discovered a chiropractic miracle worker? Or the fastest and cheapest drycleaner? Didn't you tell every one of your friends who could use the service?

By asking a customer for a testimonial, you are asking for their assistance in the growth of your business. When they feel they are truly helping and participating in the development of your company, their sense of pride will mean continuous loyalty to your product or service.

11 Ways to Get Great Testimonials

Testimonials are powerful – no question. But how do you make sure that the quotes you get from your customers will bring you the most value? How do you ensure that your client will articulate your product's merits in a clear and easy to understand way? How do you make sure you can actually use their testimonials in your marketing materials?

Asking for testimonials requires more effort than merely soliciting general comments and praise. You want to ensure that your customer feels a sense of pride and loyalty in providing their opinion, and that their opinion will have an impact on potential buyers.

How? Glad you asked. Here are 11 proven ways to get great testimonials from your customers.

1. Don't wait!

Your customers are the happiest and most willing to help you within a day to a week of their purchase, so aim to secure the testimonial in this time period. Ask for the testimonial before they leave, and make sure you have all their contact details to follow up with. This also ensures you stay on top of your testimonial recruitment!

2. Get specific

Specific testimonials are more believable. The more specific you can have your customer be, the stronger and more impactful the testimonial will be. Remember the Sleep Country testimonials that referenced the little "booties" that their delivery men wore to keep carpets clean? Meaningful details get remembered. Ask for mention of things like time, dates, extraordinary customer service, and personal observations.

3. If you were the solution – what was the problem?

Testimonials that tell stories are more engaging. Ask client to not only describe their experience with your company, but also the negative experience that led them to your door. If they can describe the struggles and challenges they were facing before receiving your service, the reader will likely be able to sympathize and resonate with similar struggles. This will motivate them to solve their problems with your solution.

4. Write the first draft

Make it easy for your clients. This technique is something you can offer someone who is hesitant to commit to writing a testimonial due to time constraints, or is procrastinating. Ask them to brainstorm a few notes they would like to include in their feedback, write them down, and string them into a concise testimonial for their review. All they have to do is review, print on their letterhead, sign, and mail back to you!

5. Include your marketing message or USP

Always ask your customers to include your unique selling proposition (USP) in the testimonial. For instance, if your USP includes exceptional customer service, same-day installation, and a money-back guarantee then ask your customer to attest to those qualities.

6. A picture says...

Yes, you know the saying. But it's true. When readers attach an image of the speaker to words, the words are enlivened and have twice as much validity and impact. When readers see an image of a previous client using your product or service, their words and opinions are even more believable. You can take these simple pictures yourself – and take many so you have a selection to choose from.

7. Credentials equal trust

As we mentioned, testimonials from credible sources will have the most believability and impact. When you ask for a testimonial, make sure your customer states their expertise and credentials. If you sell custom orthotics, and can secure a solid testimonial from a doctor, their words will be golden in your marketing materials.

8. Don't forget to ask permission

When you ask for testimonials, make sure you are clear that their words may be used in your marketing materials, including advertisements, website and in-store displays. This is a good time to thank them for their time and sincerity, and show your appreciation for their words.

9. Location, location…

Depending on the market reach of your business, the location of your customers is an important part of the believability of your testimonial. If you own a community-based business, when potential clients see you've made others happy just down their street they'll be motivated to use your service too. If you own a regional business, then the cities and addresses of other happy customers can help communicate the reach of your service.

10. Testimonials are not surveys

Keep the purpose of your request in mind when you're asking for testimonials. Testimonials should be positive fodder for your advertising materials. Surveys are used to solicit meaningful (and often confidential) customer information to refine and improve your service. Testimonials are public statements, while surveys are often anonymous and can produce less-than-positive results.

11. Say thank you!

Thanking a customer for their time and effort creating your testimonial is just plain good manners. It also increases loyalty and goodwill. This can be done via email, but sending a formal letter on your letterhead is a more meaningful approach.

Using Testimonials Strategically

So now you have a pile of glowing customer testimonials. What's next?

Choose the most powerful piece of the testimonial

What is the most convincing aspect of the testimonial? Is it the author? Where they are from? A specific sentence or paragraph they wrote? Be strategic about the aspect of the testimonial that you feature, and select what will have the most impact.

For example, you can compile a list titled *What Customers are Saying*, and list only the phrases that support your specific marketing message. Or you can feature the unique credentials or story of your customer, before you even include their testimonial. You can also summarize the testimonial with a powerful headline.

Put them on your website

Adding a page of testimonials to your website is a great start, especially when you're beginning to solicit customer responses. However, the most powerful way to ensure site visitors actually see your testimonials is to include them on every page – especially the ones with the highest traffic.

A testimonial should be placed wherever you make a strong statement about your service or product, and wherever the service or product is described. This is a great way to break up your sales copy with some "proof". As they read about your offering, your credibility will be validated by someone other than you.

Compile your best 25 to 50 letters in a display book

Like a proud grandparent, keep a book of testimonials in the waiting area of your office, your boardroom, and in your desk. Or, put one at the service counter, cash register and anywhere else people may have a moment to flip through.

I've seen this done in recruiting firm, a hardware store, and a physiotherapist's office. When clients have a chance to read the positive experiences of others, they will be more open to hearing your sales pitch less guarded when responding to your unique offering.

Hang your favorite testimonials in your store or office

Testimonials as art! Frame your favorite testimonials – preferably the ones written on client letterhead – and post them on the wall in your business. Even if clients don't read them up close, the volume and visual recognition of client logos will have impact. Plus – your next satisfied clients will want to see their company names on the wall too.

Put them in your advertisements

Use short, clear, concise testimonials in your advertising. When was the last time you saw a prescription drug advertisement without a testimonial? Can't remember? That's because you haven't. The best advertisers know that testimonials are the fastest and most effective way to overcome skepticism and get clients thinking that your product or service is the solution to their problem.

Include a page of testimonials in your direct mail

When sending your marketing materials directly to a mass list of potential clients, let the words of others speak to the merits of your product or service. Put together a page or two of testimonials, and attach it to your mailing. The credibility of your company will be instantly established, encouraging clients to act – and buy – faster.

Partner with an associate for joint mailing

If you have an associate or colleague who has a similar customer base of new prospects for your business, try a joint-endorsed mailing. Each of you will send a letter to your own clients, endorsing the other's products and services. Your service or solution is offered to a potential client by a trusted source, and you are offering your existing clients the added value of an associate's service to complement your own.

Testimonial Request Letter

Here is an example of a basic testimonial request letter that can be customized and made into a template for your unique business. This can also be sent over email if that is how your clients prefer to be contacted.

Mr. John Smith
1234 Main Street
Anytown, Anyplace 90210

January 2, 2006

Dear Mr. Smith,

Thank you for visiting our store this week. It was a pleasure helping you select a new laptop for your daughter to use at university this fall – they just grow up too fast! Your research and clear idea of the product you were searching for truly made our job easy. We love the back to school season, because it means working with clients like yourself.

We know there are a lot of choices when it comes to purchasing a laptop in Anytown, so thank you for choosing ABC Company. If there is anything else we can assist you with, please don't hesitate to contact me directly.

We occasionally ask select customers for their feedback in the form of a testimonial. Because we are so proud of the feedback we receive, we often use our customer's quotes in our marketing materials – specifically our website and sales brochures. The real life experiences of our customers at ABC Company are stories that we are proud of.

Could I ask you to write down some of your feedback? A few words about your experience with ABC Company, and how we helped you and your daughter would be greatly appreciated. We encourage you to print this on your company letterhead, so we can provide your own company with some exposure as well.

You may want to include the names of the associates who helped you, and how your daughter is enjoying her laptop. Again, we would like to feature your name and experience in our marketing materials. For your convenience, I've included a prepaid envelope with which to mail your testimonial back to us.

Thank you very much for your assistance.

Kind regards,

Your name here

Testimonial Thank You Letter

Here is an example of a short thank you letter for a testimonial that can also be customized and made into a template for your unique business. You may wish to write your thank you letters on company note cards, but try to avoid sending these thank you's via email.

Mr. John Smith
1234 Main Street
Anytown, Anyplace 90210

January 10, 2006

Dear Mr. Smith,

We received your glowing testimonial in the mail today, and I wanted to thank you personally for your kind words. Your comments about our store and our people are important to us, and I will make sure my staff takes a moment to read your letter.

We are thrilled that your daughter is enjoying her laptop, and using it to keep in touch with you while she studies abroad. When we sold it to you, we truly believed it would provide the most long-lasting value for her student budget. I hope it serves her for the rest of her time at school.

Thank you again for taking the time to write us. We are all proud to have been of service to you and your daughter, and look forward to seeing you both again soon.

Warm regards,

Your Name Here

Testimonial Examples

Below you will find a series of sample testimonials, and excerpts from testimonial letters. Read these over, and take a moment to notice why each is a powerful statement. We have also summarized each testimonial with a headline.

24% Response Rate from a Single Direct Mailing!

We were skeptical about direct mail campaigns, and unsure about the return on investment. Your strategic advice and logistical help made the project run smoothly and easily – we received over 200 leads from this single effort!

John and Betty McFee
Scottsdale, AZ

Best Sleep in 20 Years!

I can't tell you how much I appreciated Craig's patience and assistance in my mattress selection. He is so knowledgeable of each mattress' design and features, and helped us find a financing solution that worked with our budget. I haven't slept this well in over two decades. Promote him!
Jason Carmichael

Gentle and effective approach

I have always been reluctant to visit a chiropractor for my lower back pain because I am not comfortable with physical adjustments. Sarah took the time to clearly explain the cause of my pain, and gave me easy exercises to help correct the problem. She respected my comfort level, and treated me without uncomfortable cracks and snaps!

Wally Orton

Testimonial Worksheet

Start today! Brainstorm a list of recent customers and clients who you will approach for testimonials. Post this worksheet in your office, and track your progress. Aim for 50 testimonials in two months. You can never have too many.

Name + Phone	Request Letter Sent	Follow Up Call Made	Testimonial Received	Thank-you Letter Sent
	☐	☐	☐	☐
	☐	☐	☐	☐
	☐	☐	☐	☐
	☐	☐	☐	☐
	☐	☐	☐	☐
	☐	☐	☐	☐
	☐	☐	☐	☐
	☐	☐	☐	☐
	☐	☐	☐	☐
	☐	☐	☐	☐
	☐	☐	☐	☐
	☐	☐	☐	☐
	☐	☐	☐	☐
	☐	☐	☐	☐
	☐	☐	☐	☐
	☐	☐	☐	☐
	☐	☐	☐	☐
	☐	☐	☐	☐

To learn the 3 biggest mistakes all business owners make and how to avoid them, visit www.resultsorientedcoaching.com

10

Profits and Leads through Host Beneficiary Relationships

Did you know that a business just down the street from yours may be able to help double your profits this year? Or does this sound a little too farfetched?

Maybe. If you operate a retail store that sells tires, and the business down the road is a hair salon, you may have a hard time making this happen. However, loose partnerships between complementary, non-competing businesses can be a financial goldmine when implemented strategically. And your partner may be just steps away!

Formally called Host Beneficiary Relationships, these partnerships help small and medium-sized businesses tap into very specific target markets and close sales under existing relationships of trust.

HB Relationships allow one business (the 'host') to add value to their product or service, and the other (the 'beneficiary') to benefit from the impact of a referral. The beauty of this arrangement is that the roles can then be swapped; the 'host' becomes the 'beneficiary' and vice versa.

Like any marketing strategy, HB Relationships don't work for every business all the time. However, they are a great tool to keep in your marketing arsenal when starting a business, entering new markets, boosting product sales, or any other opportunity that requires a specific and personal approach.

How Can a HB Relationship Help Your Business?

Establishing, planning, and implementing a successful HB Relationship campaign is more complex than asking your neighbor to send a letter to his client base with an offer from your company.

As with every other component of your marketing strategy and materials, an HB Relationship campaign must be purpose-driven and evaluated to be the best approach to secure your desired results.

For example, if your business caters to a broad audience and you have an irresistible offer that is going to have people running through your doors, you may want to consider a simple advertisement that will reach the most people. Alternately, if you offer a common product with a low price point – like coffee or candy – it's unlikely that a HB Relationship is worth the cost and effort involved.

So in what cases will a Host Beneficiary Relationship benefit your business?

1. A Start-up Company

A company that is just starting out has the most to gain from a HB Relationship. Faced with the standard challenges of establishing a new operation – credibility, product positioning, target market establishment, marketing strategy, etc. – a HB Relationship is an ideal way to get the business off the ground.

Gaining access to a time-crafted list of potential clients in your target market is an impressive benefit. Getting an established business to communicate your offer on your behalf is an almost guaranteed way to establish your own credibility.

However, start-ups often have the least to offer a 'host' company in exchange for being the 'beneficiary'. Trading client lists is not an option in this case. So what's in it for the 'host'?

The host is seen in the eyes of his customers as providing a reward or an exclusive offer for their continued support and loyalty. The host business earns goodwill and has an excuse to contact his database for the cost of a simple mailing.

2. Entering a New Market

An established business venturing into new territory is in a prime position to benefit from a HB Relationship. Whether the business is known or unknown in the community, tapping into a refined target list will ensure that the right people are communicated the benefits of the new business' offering.

In exchange, the host business may benefit from either the beneficiary's client lists in other marketplaces, or the prestige of offering clients an exclusive offer for a new business in town.

Again, this works best when the target market is highly segmented; otherwise, an advertisement would be a faster and more cost effective strategy.

3. A New Product / Service

As with new marketplaces, launching a new product or service may require tapping into a new or more segmented audience to deliver your message. A HB Relationship with the right partner will help to correctly position your offering, and deliver it to an exact audience.

The host business benefits by offering loyal clients the first opportunity to purchase or use the beneficiary business' product or service.

Defining Your Target Market

This is crucial in establishing a HB Relationship – just like it is crucial in every other aspect of your marketing plan. Not knowing and understanding your target market will put you on the fast track to business hardship, and waste time and money in the process.

You can determine your target market – or target market segment – based on the purpose or intention for seeking a HB Relationship. Are you reaching out to a new segment of your market? Are you offering a new product or service that may appeal to a specific segment of your market? Are you moving to a new market area and looking to establish yourself amongst your broader target?

Determine your audience and write your target market here:

_____

_____

_____

Selecting a Host Business

Once you have an idea of who your target market is, you can begin to create a list of target host businesses to approach.

Not every business is going to be interested or willing to engage in this marketing strategy – so doing a little bit of research and positioning your offer is well worth your while. To begin, you will want to draft a long list of all potential host businesses.

Do this by considering all business types that would be complementary to – but not competing with – your business.

Those businesses that offer a service or product that is connected in some way to your own. For example, if you operate a hair salon, some potential HB partners would include esthetics salons, clothing stores, drug stores, and perhaps some specialty goods stores.

Or, if you operate a retail tire store, you might consider a list that includes hardware stores, automotive part shops, car washes, auto body shops, or specialty auto part distributors.

Pick up the yellow pages, or conduct a Google search for all businesses in your market area that fall under the categories you identified. You may also consider asking your colleagues and associates for ideas and recommendations.

When creating this list, make sure each business falls under these criteria:

Non-competitive. Their offer should be complementary to, but not compete with, your product or service. Make sure you consider this carefully – seemingly non-competitive offers may actually cannibalize your business.

Remember that your customers have a limited amount of money to spend, and if they begin spending money at your host's business, they might stop spending money at your business.

Same target market. If you and your host business are not talking to the same customer base, then you're wasting your words on customers who are not likely to buy your service or product. If your host business has no idea who their target market is, you may also want to consider looking at other host options.

Start with your customers – your target market or segment of. What services do they use? What products are they interested in? Thinking about their needs will help lead you to the most effective host business.

A killer customer contact list. Without this, they aren't worth approaching – but how do you know they have or maintain a customer database? There are a couple of ways. Pay attention to the type of marketing your potential host conducts. Do they often send letters to their target market? Direct-mail flyers and other promotional materials? Or do they rely on advertising? Do they send a regular newsletter? They also may hold their customer contact information in their point of sale system – if it is technologically advanced enough to do so.

Positive reputation. As the beneficiary, you need to ensure that the host who is referring your business to their customers enjoys a good reputation in the community and with its clientele. Otherwise, you are being endorsed by a business that no one respects, which can be damaging for your reputation.

Host Business Ideas List

Keep track of all potential host businesses using this chart.

Business Name	Contact	Business Type
	Name: Phone:	
	Name: Phone:	
	Name: Phone:	
	Name: Phone:	
	Name: Phone:	
	Name: Phone:	
	Name: Phone:	
	Name: Phone:	

Approaching the Host Business

Once you have created a list of target businesses, it is time to plan your approach. There is some strategy involved in this; you need to convince the host businesses to lend their endorsement and customer contact list to you in exchange for something that will benefit them.

Introduce your product or service. Present your offering to the host business as though you were presenting to your potential customers: heavy on benefits, and light on features. Assume that the host business has placed themselves in the shoes of their customers, and is evaluating whether your product or service is worthwhile for them.

Provide marketing materials and other supporting information like testimonials and market research to establish your credibility, and your understanding of the people you are trying to reach.

Inform and excite. Provide as much information about how the HB Relationship will work, and be sincere in your efforts. Leave room for their thoughts and contributions to ensure that they buy into the process.

Get them excited about the opportunity you've placed in front of them. Use bright examples, and tell a hypothetical story about one of their customers benefiting from your service. Then, bring it back to the benefits that the relationship or partnership will deliver to their business.

Include an incentive. Be clear about the benefits the host can expect to receive. While you will not always be able to offer something tangible, do your best to offer some incentive to the prospective host business.

If you are an established business, offer them reverse access to your customer database after the initial mailing. Or, if you have room in your margin, offer them a piece of the profits you receive from their customers. Whatever it is, make sure you articulate how this particular partnership is worth their while.

Communicate your rationale. Tell the host why you chose to approach them in particular. Do they enjoy a great reputation in the community? Are they a well-known business with a great sense of camaraderie? Compliment them on their business skills and the great relationships they have built with their customers and in the community.

Then, explain how your business can add value to theirs, and allow them to build on the existing relationships with their clients by offering your services.

Reassure. Communicate the benefits of the HB Relationship to the host, and reassure them that there is no risk involved for them. You are not out to take their profits, or place burden on their resources.

Remind them that you are seeking a complementary business relationship, one that benefits both parties.

Craft Your Message

Once you have secured your host partner, put the plan into action as quickly as possible. Offering to write the letter to their customers will not only give you control over the messaging of the offer, but also reduce the time investment required by the host. The process is simplified for them, and happens sooner for you.

- Just like sales letters and other marketing collateral, your HB offer letter should engage the reader and make them feel as though their needs and interests are cared for.

- The letter should position the host as a thoughtful service provider who sought out an offer specifically for the target audience.

- Your offer should be strong and slightly outrageous. Give deep discounts, or free services, exclusively to this target audience.

- Remember to acknowledge the needs and troubles of your reader, and position your product or service as the answer or solution.

- Include an incentive to act quickly. Ensure your offer is time-sensitive or of limited quantity.

Five Simple Steps to Creating an HB Relationship

In summary, here are is a five-step roadmap to creating a positive, profit-filled, HB Relationship:

- Identify your target market.
- Identify target host businesses.

- Create a unique offer for each host business.
- Approach the host business.

Draft your letter.

Points to Remember

- **Make mistakes in small batches.** If you are unsure about the accuracy of your target market – do a test run. Send a small batch of 50-100 letters to a small group of people, and measure the response.

    - Alternately, you can send three different letters to each third of your target market, and evaluate which offer is acted on the most. This is of benefit for both the host and the beneficiary business because the response rate of the target market is tested, as are their purchase motivations.

- **Create benefit for the host business.** Remember that there must be an incentive for the host business, or the partnership is not worth the time investment. It is important to consider this, and plan ahead before you approach the host business. Create a number of options for the host to choose from, whether it is using your database after the initial mailing, or sharing a piece of the profits.

- **Be honest.** If you are working with several businesses in your area on different offers, make sure each business knows and is comfortable with the arrangement. Ensure that each offer is distinctive and each host is benefiting from the arrangement without competing with other host businesses. This is just good business form.

- **Rest on the strength of your offer.** With a strong offer, your HB campaign will be on the path to success. Make it something your audience can't refuse. Your offer should not only be enticing and engaging for your audience, but should also benefit the host in reputation. Their customers should feel valued and appreciative toward the host for bringing your offer forward.

- **Repeat.** Once you've established one successful HB partnership, keep going! This technique is a valuable way to promote your business and your unique products and services, and can be repeated several times each year with several different host businesses.

Host Beneficiary Letter Template

[Headline in bold at the top of the page – strong statement or question] [Optional sub headline to explain or answer the question/statement]

To learn the 3 biggest mistakes all business owners make and how to avoid them, visit www.resultsorientedcoaching.com

Dear [name],

I hope this letter finds you well and enjoying [insert name or description of product or service previously purchased]. Remember, your continued satisfaction with our [product or service] is guaranteed.

I am writing because I have stumbled upon an exclusive new [product or service] that will [describe how the product or service will meet a need or solve a problem].

[Beneficiary business name] is a [describe business type] that [describe business function]. I recently met with the owner, and was able to secure an unbelievable rate for my existing clients. The [product or service] is [describe product or service briefly]. Customers who have already purchased have said:
[list testimonials in bullet form]

[describe limited time or quantity], we are pleased to offer you [describe unique offer here]. This is an opportunity you will not find anywhere else, and an offer that will not be available in stores.

I hope you will be able to take advantage of this amazing [product or service].

Sincerely,
[your name]
[company name]
[phone number]

HB Relationship Worksheet

Target Market:	
Potential Host 1: Name: Business Type:	**Unique Offer:**
Host Benefits:	**Date Contacted:**
	☐ Accepted ☐ Follow-up
Notes:	

Target Market:	
Potential Host 2: Name: Business Type:	**Unique Offer:**
Host Benefits:	**Date Contacted:**
	☐ Accepted ☐ Follow-up
Notes:	

So What Do You Do From Here?

Take Action! If you're already an accomplished business owner and earning in excess of $250,000.00 per year (rich according to the Federal Government), use this book as direction to enhance the speed of your business success. If you are not as accomplished as you would like to be then the smartest thing to do is…

A) Remove the fear of failure by not taking action
B) Make the first step
C) Be consistent and persistent
D) Stay the course and the success will follow

Concentrate on strategies to LEARN and the EARN will follow! If you are serious about taking the next step then go to work on yourself, study other business successes, understand marketing strategies and become a sponge for new (proven) material. The amazing thing about the game of business is that when you put proven processes to work and continue to follow them, an abundance of success will follow. The biggest mistake is to start a process and then fallback into your old habits after a short time.

Above all, get the knowledge you need before you step onto the field. Think about it… if you were going to challenge Michael Jordan to a game of H O R S E for money, wouldn't it make sense to learn the game and practice before you stepped on the court to play him? It is amazing to me how many new small business people start the game of business against seasoned professionals (the competition), without first developing the necessary knowledge to be successful. Then they fail and blame the market, the economy, their location, etc.

If you have a business and have not yet managed to start to create wealth and systems that allow you to take time off, build retirement accounts or pay for your children's college, then learn and master the steps outlined in my book. I am a huge advocate of education and mentorships. Get the right information, find someone that knows how to walk you through them and watch your quality of life take new shape.

To learn how to avoid the 3 key mistakes all small business owners make, visit www.resultsorientedcoaching.com

Made in the USA
Lexington, KY
22 December 2017